Best Types of Gold and Silver for Investments

Discover if Silver is Better than Gold, are Gold Coins Better Than Gold Bars, are Silver Bars Better Than Silver Coins, are Numismatic Coins a Smart Choice, Does Junk Silver Make a Wise Investment and Much, Much More.

DOYLE SHULER

Copyright Notice

Table of Contents

Introduction

Congratulations on making a wise decision to read this book and educate yourself about precious metals investing. There are so many new precious metals investors who jump in and start buying like crazy before they know what they are doing or why they are doing it. Hopefully this does not describe you.

This book is written for new to moderate level precious metals investors who want to be sure they are making the right choices for the right reasons. I will keep the information on a pretty high level. Most people just want to understand the basics and then get started. They don't have the time nor the desire to learn every single tidbit of information there is to know about precious metals. It's like when someone asks you what time it is, they just want to know the time, they don't what to know how the watch works.

So that's my promise to you. I will keep the information in this book short and to the point. I also will not try and impress you with a lot of complicated terms and tech-speak. I will keep it simple and easy to understand. The information in this book is laid out in a very logical and practical way and is designed to help you make wise investing decisions quickly.

Like many metals investors, I have gotten much of my education from the school of hard knocks and mistakes. I have been ripped off and made poor buying decisions more than I care to admit. However, those mistakes have taught me valuable lessons and I truly hope that I can help you avoid making many of the poor decisions that I have made.

Over decades of metals investing I have discovered the good programs, the bad programs and the ugly programs. At the end of this book you will find a **Resource** section that has a number of programs that I have discovered over the years that deserve an A+ and I wanted to share them with you. Hopefully they will save you a lot of time, money and frustration.

Okay then. Are you ready? Then let's get started.

Disclaimer

I want to let you know upfront that I am not a financial advisor, a financial planner, nor a licensed investment broker. I am not giving financial or investment advice in this book. I have been a precious metals investor for almost 30 years and have learned quite a bit on the subject. It seems that so much of the information about precious metals is given by people who are trying to sell you the metals they have. Much of the information out there is bias and slanted towards their benefit. My goal here is to give you a simple, non-bias, basic to moderate educational understanding of precious metals so that you can make smart investment decisions for you and your family. You should always seek the advice of competent investment professionals before making any investment decisions. All investment have risk and precious metals are no exception. You can lose money with precious metals. Always do your own due diligence before making any investment decision.

Define Your Investment Goals

Before you decide which metals are best for you to purchase, you should first stop and analyze your investment goals and reasons for buying metals. This will definitely make a difference in which types of metals are right for you. Why do you want to buy precious metals in the first place? Here are some popular reasons that many people have for buying precious metals:

> They want to protect their assets from the possible decline or collapse of the currency.

> They want to protect their assets from inflation.

> They simply want to diversify their investment portfolio.

> They want to put some of their assets into *"private"* holdings.

> They want to buy and sell on short term price moves to try and profit from market moves.

> They see metals as one of the few investment options that has the greatest chance of appreciation in the future.

> They want to diversify their *"fiat currency based"* portfolio with real, actual, tangible assets.

- ➢ They want to buy and hold so they will have a fallback position in case the "worst case" economic scenario happens.

- ➢ They have a strong distrust of the Government and want to stay off of the grid as much as possible.

- ➢ They don't trust the banks and want to put their money into something they do trust.

- ➢ They fear the worst and want to have metals to use for possible barter if things get really bad.

- ➢ Their brother in law told them they should buy some metals.

- ➢ They like bright and shiny objects......

The list can go on forever, but I am sure you get the point. It's important that you know *your* reasons for wanting to buy the metals in the first place. Once you get clear on your reasons, you will find it much easier to decide which types of metals are right for you.

How Much
Do You Have To Invest

While this may seem like an odd question to ask, it is actually very relevant. I receive calls pretty often from people who are brand new to precious metals investing. Some of them don't have a clue as to what to buy, so they ask me what I suggest. One of the first questions I have for them is, about how much do you have to invest. Some of them are initially taken back by the question. As the conversation progresses, they begin to understand why I asked the question in the first place, because it does make a difference.

When it comes to deciding which metals you should invest in, a great deal depends on how much money you have to invest. Basically, the more money you have to invest in precious metals, the more you can afford to diversify your holdings.

Think of it this way. I will use a traditional investment example of stocks, bonds, equities, etc. If you are Warren Buffett and have untold billions to invest, then you can and should be widely diversified and own a very large baskets of investment holdings so that you can diversify your holding and your risk. There is no reason not to own a wide variety of individual stocks, bonds,

ETFs, as well as owning entire companies in many different industries, and much, much more. If you can afford it, it's the smart way to invest.

On the other hand, if you only have a few thousand dollars to invest, then your diversification options will be very limited and it will have a big influence on what you can and cannot invest in. The same concept holds true for precious metals.

The more money you have to invest, the greater your options. In most cases, it pays to diversify. Since none of us knows what the economic future holds, diversifying your precious metals holdings is the smart way to go. We will take a look at the various diversification options as we continue.

Asset Allocation

The next obvious question that comes up is, *"What percentage of my investment portfolio should I have in precious metals?"* Good question. Let me caution you here. If you go out and ask people this question, the answers you receive will often be biased by who you ask. If you ask a traditional stock broker or financial planner who is not able to sell you any physical precious metals, you can bet they will likely give you a very, very low amount if any at all.

Clearly not all stock brokers and financial planners would do this but unfortunately some will often try and steer you towards "paper" gold and silver investments in the form of mutual funds, ETFs, mining stocks, etc. The reason many of them will steer you towards them is because;

(1) They have the ability to sell them to you.

(2) They can make a profit on them when they sell them.

(3) They understand them and that's what they are knowledgeable about.

After all, you wouldn't think to ask a BMW dealer if he thinks you should by a Mercedes, would you? Pretty simple, right? It works the exact same way with investments. (Heck, it even works the same way with health care. I recently got a cold hard lesson on this, but that's another story for another time.)

On the other hand, if you ask a precious metals broker/dealer this question, they will likely give you a very large suggested percentage of metals to own because it is in their best interest for you to buy more from them. The more you buy from them, the more they make. So with all of this confusion and bias out there, how do you decide what percentage is right for you?

At the end of the day, it really comes down to what you are comfortable with. These days the most popular opinion seems to be that you should have anywhere from 5% to 10% of your investment portfolio in physical gold and silver. I personally know some very high level financial planners who only deal with 7 and 8 figure clients, and they suggest their clients have 40%+ in physical gold and silver. Are they right? Who knows? However, do keep in mind our discussion about how much money you have. What's right for a high net worth investor is not always right for a low net worth investor.

I strongly suggest that you don't put all of your investment eggs in one basket. It always pays to diversify your holdings because no one ever knows what will happen next and which investments will soar and which ones will get creamed. Even if you believe that the metals prices are going to the moon, you should still diversify and not put all of your holding into metals.

Also, keep this in mind. As long as you buy the right types of metals, they are really easy to buy and sell. You don't have to stress out over your asset allocation percentage like it's a permanent decision. You can ramp your percentage of metals up or down pretty quickly. I believe the key is to go ahead and at least get some of your portfolio into physical precious metals and then you can adjust the percentage as you go.

Physical vs Non-Physical

Most likely if you are reading this book, you already know that you want to buy physical metals instead of non-physical metals. However, we will touch on this subject briefly just in case you have some questions here. Again, depending on who you ask, some people will try and persuade you to buy non-physical precious metals. Non-physical precious metals can be in the form of investments like; mutual funds, exchange traded funds (ETFs), mining stocks, certificates, etc. that are involved with some form of precious metals.

Their argument will be, *"When you buy these types of non-physical precious metals you can buy and sell them quickly and easily, you don't have to worry about having them shipped to you, you don't have to worry about storing them, and you don't have to worry about someone knocking you in the head and taking them from you."* They will tell you that these investments are just as good or better than that old "physical" gold and silver.

While most of the above arguments may be true, they don't take into account the other side of the coin, so to speak. They don't tell you what happens to the value of those investment options if the stock market crashes, if the currency fails, if we have significant inflation, or a myriad of other possible economic scenarios that could cause the value of those investments to plummet.

Many people these days often say this about gold and silver; *"If you can't hold it, touch it, feel it and have physical possession of it... it ain't real."* I must say, I totally agree with them. If you own physical gold and silver, then you own a something that has maintained a store of value for centuries. People have fought and died for it. Countries have gone to war over it. Physical gold and silver have stood the test of time and have always come out a winner. You can also go to sleep at night knowing that there will never come a day when you wake up and discover that your physical gold and silver is worth nothing.

There is simply no substitute for the actual, real, physical metals. Have you ever held any physical gold or silver in your hands? If not, you should. It's hard to describe the feeling, but it is pretty amazing. It just does something to people. You get the since that it is real. That it is valuable. It's always fun to be with someone who has never held any physical metals in their hands before. I ask them to hold out their hand, I then place a silver or gold coin in their hand, and watch their face. It's amazing to watch their expression. It really does have a noticeable impact on most people the first time they experience it.

So my advice is... at least buy some physical precious metals. Don't fake yourself out by only owning paper metals. After all, paper is still paper, and physical precious metals are still the real thing.

The Basics

Okay, before we dig into the real meat of this, let's take a moment and review some of the basics so you won't be lost as we move forward. Here are some basic terms that are very important to know when it comes to investing in precious metals:

BULLION: Many people get confused about this term. Some think it is used to describe pirate treasure. The term bullion is used to describe gold, silver, platinum or palladium coins which closely follow market spot prices and have little or no numismatic value. The term is also used to describe the form in which metal is shaped such as bars, ingots or wafers.

SPOT PRICE: This is a big one that is critical to know. Spot price is the current, real-time market price of the precious metal. There are hundreds of websites that show the current spot prices. When you buy or sell precious metals, the price is always based off of the spot price. You can find lots of Apps and websites that make it easy for you to watch the spot price of metals 24/7. Here is just one place that you can instantly see the current spot price of all precious metals, including historical price charts: www.GoldSilverAlliance.com

MARGIN or PREMIUM: These terms are used to describe the difference between what a broker/dealer will charge to sell or buy a precious metals item. When buying or selling metals, the price is usually made up of the current Spot Price plus the Premium or Margin amount that the broker/dealer is charging. This amount can include the costs of fabrication, distribution and the broker/dealer fees. That is how the broker/dealer makes their profit, by adding their premium or margin amount to the transaction. The lower the premium or margin amount, the better it is for you and the more affordable the metals will be.

TROY OUNCE: This is the traditional unit of weight used for precious metals.

FIAT MONEY: Paper money that is made legal tender by Government law, although it is not backed by gold or silver.

LEGAL TENDER: This is a coin or currency that is identified by a Government to be an acceptable form in the discharging of debts.

MINT: A place where coins or bars are manufactured.

NUMISMATIC COINS: Coins whose prices depend more on their rarity, condition, dates, and mint marks than they depend on their gold or silver content, if any.

ASK PRICE: The price at which a dealer offers to sell items to you.

BID PRICE: The price at which a dealer offers to buy items from you.

Okay, I think that is enough basic information to get us started. Let's move on.

How Much Space Will Your Metals Take Up

This is something that many brand new metals investors simply do not know. Before you decide which metals to invest in, you should have some idea of just how much space they will take up and where you plan to store them. I had a medical doctor call me a few years ago with some questions about storage. This doctor had been searching various warehouses in his local area to try and find a suitable location to store his gold in. His question to me was, about how many square feet of storage space he would need to store all the gold he was getting ready to buy.

My first response was, *"My goodness doc... how much gold are you planning on buying?"* He told me he was going to start with $600,000 worth of gold, but was very concerned with how much space it would take up. I did a quick calculation in my head and then I answered his question. (Before I tell you, would you like to take a guess?)

I told him that if he had on a normal pair of pants, with good size pockets, and if he were to purchase gold bars (which are very compact), he could practically put all $600,000 worth of gold in his front and back pants pockets. (Yes it would be a tight squeeze and yes it would be very heavy, about 24 pounds, but to make a point, you could do it.) There was a long pause on the phone… total silence. Finally he broke the silence and said, you have got to be kidding me. Nope. It's true. Gold is a very private and very portable source of wealth, and you usually don't need a warehouse to store it in.

On the other hand, silver can take up quite a bit of space. For example, if you were to buy $600,000 worth of silver, let's see how much space it would take up. Let's say you decided to buy the American Silver Eagle 1 ounce coins. 500 coins come from the US Mint in a convenient green plastic box called a monster box. At the current price of silver eagles as I am writing this book, you would need about 38 monster boxes. Each box is 15 inches long by 8.5 inches wide and 4.5 inches tall and they weigh about 43 pounds each. 38 monster boxes would weigh about 1,634 pounds. (Don't try and put that in your pants pockets.)

There are lots of different storage options available and we will discuss them later on in the book, but if you plan on storing your metals in your home or office, then you should at least give some thought to the space issue.

What Type of
Precious Metal Is Best

Now we come to the BIG question that everyone wants to know. *"What type of metals are best to buy? Is gold better than silver? Which metal is the best?"* Well that's another good question with no simple answer.

Basically there are 4 main precious metals; gold, silver, platinum and palladium. There are some very vocal investors who are very bullish on platinum and palladium and strongly recommend it. As I promised in the beginning, I will keep to the basics and keep this book very main stream. If you are interested in platinum and palladium, I'm sure there is a lot of good information about them that's widely available, but I will not focus on them here.

Without a doubt, gold and silver are by far the two most followed, most popular and most purchased and sold precious metals. Both make excellent investments. Now that we are focusing on just gold and silver, which one of these metals makes for the "best" investment for you?

As I am sure you know, the answer to this question depends on who you ask. Yes, there are gold bugs out there who only buy gold and nothing else. Likewise, there are silver investors out there who are silver through and through and don't go near gold. However, keep in mind what we covered earlier about diversification. If you have a good size sum to invest, then without a doubt, it's best to diversify and buy some of both.

If your dollar amount to invest is low, then you have fewer options. Typically silver is a great place to start with if your budget is limited. It is sometimes referred to as *"poor man's gold."*

Let's take a quick look at the fundamentals of each of these amazing metals.

Why Consider Investing in Gold?

– Gold is the only form of money that has never failed in the 5,000 year history of it being used by mankind.

– Currently, there is only enough investment-grade gold available on Earth today for every living person to have 1/3rd of an ounce.

– Throughout human history, gold has been revalued to account for all excess currency in circulation. When fiat currencies fail, gold is almost always the fallback.

– In times of crisis, gold is the safest investment that also has the greatest potential to increase in value.

– Gold can be a completely private and anonymous investment that is also extremely portable.

Why Consider Investing in Silver?

– There is currently less investment-grade silver available on Earth for investors to purchase than there is gold.

– There is only enough investment-grade silver available on Earth for every person to have 1/14th of an ounce. (And some have way more than their share. J)

– Silver is often called the 'miracle metal'. It's second only to oil as the world's most useful commodity.

– In addition to being used for money, silver has thousands of essential industrial uses. Silver is the most electrically

19

conductive, thermally resistant, and reflective metal on earth and it has no known substitutes.

—   Over the past 30 years the world has used up more silver than it has been mined. Silver inventories are now near all-time record low levels.

Those are some pretty impressive facts, and they make a great case for owning both metals. To help you better decide which metal is best for you; let's take a look at the historical silver to gold ratios.

What Is the Silver to Gold Ratio?

If you go back thousands of years in history you will discover that the free market value of silver to gold was about 12 to 1. That means that it took about 12 ounces of silver to equal the value of 1 ounce of gold. This was based on availability, that being that there was about 12 times as much silver as there was gold available. There is actually less above ground silver available today than at any time in our modern history.

In more modern times, the silver to gold ratio has averaged 16 to 1, meaning it takes an average of 16 ounces of silver to equal the value of one ounce of gold.

As I am writing this book, the current silver to gold ratio is about 56 to 1. That means that it now takes about 56 ounces of silver to equal 1 ounce of gold. While no one knows what the future holds many experts predict that the gold silver ratio will eventually swing back to its historical averages. Others predict that since the ratio has been so one sided for so long, that when it swings back, it will actually over shoot its historical average and swing to a ratio of 8 to 1 or. If you do the math here, you can easily see how the price of silver has the potential for explosive growth.

Another important thing to keep in mind is that silver is much more divisible than gold from a cost standpoint. In other words, if we one day needed to use precious metals for exchange, it would be a lot easier to exchange a silver coin instead of a gold coin. Think of it this way. If one person's wallet was filled with $1.00 bills and another person only had $100 dollar bills in their wallet, if a merchant could not "break a hundred dollar bill", then it would make it much more difficult to buy goods. The guy with the $1.00 bill would find it much easier to buy and sell.

On the other hand, if you needed to leave town fast, or leave the country fast, and you wanted to take as much of your wealth with you as you reasonably could, you could take a much, much larger sum of gold with you than you could of silver. Gold is a very dense and portable form of wealth.

Some experts predict that gold will explode in value if our currency crashes and/or if we go back to the gold standard or even to a partial gold standard. Yet others predict if or when the rate of devaluation of the currency increases, the prices of both gold and silver will soar. Then, as more *"first time"* metals investors of average means flood into the market, they will not be able to afford gold and will flock to silver, "the poor man's gold," and that added demand will cause the price of silver to soar as well.

I know this can get confusing. The truth of the matter is that no one knows exactly what will happen and how things will play out. We are truly in uncharted global economic waters and anything could happen. My advice to you is to go with your gut instinct. Do what you think is best for you and your family.

Again, the good news is that most forms of gold and silver are very liquid and very easy to sell. If you change your mind at some point, you should be able to sell off some of one metal and buy more of the other.

You may want to consider owning a percentage of both metals. I have some colleagues who buy 10% gold and 90% silver and others who buy 65% gold and 35% silver, and all ratios in-between. I can tell you that the majority of my friends and the people whom I know overwhelmingly buy a lot, lot, lot more silver than they do gold. They do this because they believe silver has a lot more explosive growth potential. There is no right or wrong. I believe it's more important to take action and at least get some metals, than to over analyze it to death and do nothing.

Understanding the Premiums and Margins for Coins & Bars

Before we dive into learning about the various coins and bars to invest in, let's take a quick look at what goes into the total cost of coins and bars.

The majority of our discussions here will be about bullion coins and bars. That means that they carry no additional value for their rarity, age, condition, etc. We are just talking about bullion here and looking at what goes into the actual cost of the various bullion items. From a value stand point, we always start with the spot price of the metal. That is the market price of the metal. In addition to the spot price, they also factor in the cost to fabricate or produce the coins or bars, the distribution costs, shipping costs and also the supply or availability premium that may or may not be added.

Someone has to buy the raw metal and form it into coins and bars. It's simply a manufacturing process. Trucks full of raw metals come in one door, and a finished product goes out the other door. In the middle is the labor and overhead cost that's required to produce the various forms of metals.

Most coins come in 1 ounce sizes, but some also come in ½ ounce, ¼ ounce and even 1/10 ounce sizes. As for bullion bars, most of them can be purchased anywhere from a fraction of a gram (for gold), up to 1 ounce, 10 ounces, 100 ounces, 1,000 ounces and even larger.

The easiest way I have found to explain this is to imagine that you are in your kitchen and you are in the baking business. I come to you and tell you that I have two orders for you. One order is for a large sheet cake, or just a large flat cake. The other order is for 1,000 cup cakes. Now I promise you I am no baker, so I have very little actual experience in this area, but common since tells you that once you mix up the cake batter, it has got to be a lot easier, a lot quicker, and a lot less expensive to simply pour all of that cake batter into one large sheet cake pan, and stick it in the oven and be done with it, right?

Compare that to having to pour out 1,000 individual cupcakes and manage to get them all poured with the correct amounts and then get all of them into the oven, bake them and then have to take all of them out of the cupcake molds, etc. This process has got to take a lot longer and cost a lot more, than simply making the one sheet cake.

That is a simple example of how making bullion coins and bars works. If you compare the cost of producing one, 1 ounce silver coin, to producing one, 1,000 ounce silver bar... or if you compare the cost of producing one, 1 ounce gold coin, to producing ten, 1/10 ounce gold coins, you know it has got to cost a lot more to produce the smaller sizes than it does to produce the larger sizes.

This additional manufacturing cost has to be covered in the markup that the manufacture charges to produce the item. So to put in it real simple terms, it will cost you more to buy ten, 1/10 ounce gold coins than it will to buy one, 1 ounce gold coin. And it will also cost you more to buy ten, 10 ounce silver bars than it will to buy one, 100 ounce silver bar. This is pretty simple but just keep this in mind as we start to look at the various bullion items.

Supply and Demand Factors

The availability of certain coins along with supply and demand dynamics can also affect the premiums and margins charged for those coins. If something is hard to get, and the demand for it is strong, then the price will go up. Compared to the size of the equities markets, the size of the metals markets is relatively small. If there is a shift in supply or demand for any given item, the price of that item will naturally be affected.

Broker / Dealer Mark Ups

Lastly, the broker/dealer markup is an important factor in the price of the metals you buy. In the USA alone there are over 10,000 metals broker/dealers. Some dealers operate on very high volumes and charge relatively low markups and others will charge whatever the market will pay. I have seen some with markups as high as 40% and more. Keep in mind that all of the bullion coins and bars are commodities. You don't get more "bang for your buck" if you pay more for them, so the less expensive you can buy them for, the better.

Also keep in mind that some dealers use every trick in the book to siphon more money from you with up-sells, cross-sells, down-sells, hidden fees & costs, processing fees, shipping fees, payment fees and much, much more. Some of the most talented and skilled sales people I have ever seen in my life have been in the precious metals industry. Many of these salespeople are GOOOOOOD salespeople. They know how to get you to do things that you otherwise would never do. My advice is to keep both eyes wide open, trust your instincts, take your time, and don't fall for the, *"You gotta decide right now"* ploy. It really pays to shop around and be sure that you always compare apples to apples and that you gather <u>ALL</u> of the added & hidden fees and charges before you buy.

The Best Types of Coins to Buy

Okay, so by now perhaps you know what type of metal you want to buy (gold or silver), but now you need to decide what form of metals to buy. Should you buy coins, bars or what? We will take them one at a time and discuss the pros and cons of the various options available. There are practically an infinite number of different gold and silver coins that you can purchase, but for the purposes of this book, we are assuming you are a fairly new metals investor so we will discuss the basic and most popular types of coins available. As you become more experienced, you can branch out into more rare and exotic coins if you wish. We will keep it simple and basic for now.

Please keep in mind that everyone has their own strong opinions on these issues. It's kind of like asking someone what is the best type of car to buy. The answer just depends on who you ask, right? Okay, let's take a look at some bullion coins.

Government Produced Coins vs Rounds

To keep this simple, there are basically two main types of bullion coins. One type is produced by a Government, and the rounds are produced by private mints. Most Governments guarantee both the purity and the weight of their coins, and this is a big deal. Also, due to coinage laws, most Governments dictate that rounds should be slightly different in diameter and thickness.

The Government produced coins are usually produced with pure silver or gold. In most cases the rounds are produced with pure silver and gold as well, however some private mints also produce some rounds and commemorative coins that are not made with pure silver and gold. They often fill them with inferior metals and put a very thin coating of actual gold or silver on the surface of the coin. These companies are experts in using carefully worded descriptions that include a lot of confusing language that most people don't understand. It keeps them legal, but it obscures the average buyer's attention from the fact they are not pure forms of gold or silver. You really need to watch out for this.

In most countries that produce their own bullion coins, the coins are actual legal tender, meaning that they can legally be used as currency in exchange for goods and services in that country. For example, a 1 ounce American Silver Eagle coin has "One Dollar" stamped on the coin. That means you could go to the grocery store, pick up a pack of gum and pay for it with a silver eagle coin that has the exchange rate value of 1 dollar. The clerk would (should) take that coin in exchange for a dollar, and give you back the appropriate amount of change.

At the time I am writing this book, the spot price of silver is around $30 an ounce so it would be foolish to spend that coin as legal tender and only receive a $1 value for it, when it is really worth over $30. You could easily sell that coin to a coin dealer and get about $30 US dollars to buy a lot more gum with.

Governments control the images stamped on their coins and they are usually very consistent with them so their coins will have instant recognition. Since rounds are produced by private mints, they can stamp any images they want on their coins. Some rounds producers are also very consistent with the images on their coins and they pattern them to *"somewhat"* resemble Government coins. However, you can't believe all of the different images that are stamped on various rounds. I have seen some with Santa Clause on them; pretty much every holiday has been represented on coins, and every type of animal imaginable. I have even seen rounds with monkeys on them.

Generally speaking, the markups or margins or premiums on rounds are less than they are for the Government produced coins. So if all you are after is being able to buy as much silver or gold as you can, for the least amount possible, in coin form, then the rounds are usually the least expensive way to go.

Keep in mind that you will usually get back the same ratio of value for the premium that you paid, when you sell your coin. No guarantees, but usually. In other words let's say we bought an American Silver Eagle coin for $3.50 over spot price and a silver round for $1.50 over spot price. That gives you a $2.00 difference between the two coins. Depending on who you sell your coins back to, what the silver market is like when you sell and various other factors, there is a good chance that you would get $2 more for the silver eagle coin than you would for the round. You should be able to recoup the premium that you paid for the coin.

There are quite a few hard core "rounds" people out there and that's all they ever buy, rounds. Some of them would think you are crazy to buy anything but rounds. However, I don't see it that way, and this is just my personal opinion. Here is how I see it.

First of all, remember what we said about how much money you have to invest and diversification? The more money you have, the more you can diversify. If you are new to investing in metals I believe you should build a core position in bullion coins produced by the country in which you live, if your country produces their own coins. If your country does not produce their own coins, I would start my core position with Government coins from either the nearest country to where you live, or from the strongest and most respected country that you can find.

If you live in the USA, I would buy the American Eagles, if you live in Canada, I would buy the Maple Leafs, in you live in Britain, buy the Britannias, if you live in Austria, buy the Philharmonics, if you live in Mexico, buy the Libertads, if you live in China, buy the Pandas, I think you get the point. Just keep it simple in the beginning.

Here is why I am such a strong believer in at least building your initial core position with coins produced and backed by Governments. At least one of the reasons many people invest in precious metals is for protection. They want to be sure that if they wake up one morning and their world is suddenly turned up-side-down and everything that was normal is no longer normal, that they will at least have their physical gold and silver to fall back on. If that scenario were to happen, and if you were

31

to have to rely on your gold and silver to get by and exchange for the things you need, I know I sure would prefer having the most well-known, most recognized bullion coins available.

If you have to rely on others to recognize and agree to take your coins as a store of value in exchange for goods and services or cash, you simply cannot rely on others to be as knowledgeable about metals as you are. I have seen some actual silver rounds with monkeys stamped on the coins. If I were in a bad situation like the one described above and if I had to trade my silver for something important, I sure as hell would not want to show up with a coin with a monkey or Santa Clause on it and expect the merchant to know what it was and know that it has a real value for its silver content.

I would much rather have a coin that was minted by the Government of the country that I live in. I would rather have a coin whose weight and purity is guaranteed by the Government who made it. I believe a Government minted coins would have the greatest likelihood of being recognized and accepted. Plus, Government coins are also legal tender in that country. To me, even if I have to pay a little more for them than I would for the silver rounds, I look at that slight price difference as I would an insurance premium. To me the peace of mind is totally worth the difference. And, it is very likely that I will get that same premium back when I go to sell my coins anyway.

Even if the worst case scenario does not happen, at some point you will probably want to sell your coins to cash in and make a profit. If you happen to sell your rounds with the monkey on them back to the same dealer whom you bought them from, then you should be okay. However, the dealer whom you buy from does not always offer the best price when you go to sell them. If you find a dealer who is offering the best prices on buying back silver, that dealer may not recognize your monkey coins and may not buy them back. Or if he does agree to buy them, he may buy them back at a discount. To me it's simply not worth it. I would rather go with a "known coin" and not worry about it.

The above information is for a worst case scenario. As long as things are "normal" most dealers would have no problem buying back rounds. I don't believe you would have much of an issue with rounds as long as market conditions and the economy are okay. However, one of the reasons many people buy metals in the first place is to protect them in worst case scenarios.

Going back to our diversification concept, after you have purchased your core holding amount of Government issued coins and you feel that you have enough of them, then I have no problem at all with you buying as many rounds as you want. In my opinion, I say; get your core amount of Government coins first, and then you can diversify and buy all of the rounds you want.

Reporting and Tax Consequences

This is another really important thing to keep in mind. You should check on the Government reporting and tax issues in your country before you make your buying decisions. This issue can be somewhat involved and complicated. To clear all of the misconceptions about this subject, I wrote a book that goes into great detail about all of the tax and reporting issues involved with the buying and selling of precious metals in the United States. If you would like to learn more on this subject you can find out much more information in the book: **How to Buy and Sell Gold & Silver Privately**. More information on this "Privacy" book can be found in the **Resources** chapter of this book.

I can tell you that if you are a United States citizen, you can buy all of the gold and silver you want and neither you nor the dealer has to report anything about your purchase to the IRS. If you choose to pay cash for them and don't want the cash transaction reported, then you must keep your purchases under $10,000. You can buy all you want with checks and bank wires and no reporting is necessary.

Then, when it comes time to sell some or all of your gold and silver, if you bought the *"right"* types of gold and silver, you can sell all you want, and the sale of the metals is not reportable to the IRS at all. Thus both the buying and selling of gold and silver can be done with complete and total privacy, if you know they right types of metals to buy. This is a really, really big deal to a lot of metals investors. Their privacy is a huge thing, so why not just go with the metals that are the most private?

Please don't confuse the above with the requirement to pay capital gains tax on your gains or profits from your precious metals sales. If you make a profit on something, the US Government wants its share of your profits and it's your responsibility to report those profits and pay the taxes. Sorry, but there is no way around this, it's the law.

The Best Types of Bars to Buy

Most Governments do not produce bullion bars. These bars are typically produced by private mints from around the world. When you start to decide which types and sizes of bars that you want to buy, there are a few main factors to consider. The first is, are you going to buy "name brand" bars or generic bars. Yep, there are lots of options and lots of choices here as well.

There are a hand full of very well know and highly respected mints that produce bullion bars. When one of these respected mints produces these bars, they either mold or stamp their company name into the form of the bar itself. Thus we call them "name brand" bars. Some of these mints will also stamp a different serial number for each bar they produce. Most will record these serial numbers to help with authentication but some do not record them. The majority of these bars are produced with 99.99% pure silver or gold and the purity is often molded or stamped onto the bar itself.

To help get you started, here is a partial list of some much respected companies that produce excellent quality bullion bars. This is neither a recommendation nor an endorsement of any of these companies. You should always do your own due diligence when buying metals.

Engelhard

Johnson Matthey

Pamp Suisse

Credit Suisse

Perth Mint

There are also a large number of private mints that produce generic bars. These are simply bars that are produced with no company name on them. They are usually made from pure gold or silver as well, they just don't have name on them.

Both name brand and generic bars are made into different sizes and shapes. Typically but not always, the name brand bars carry a slightly higher premium than the generic bars do. An analogy would be like buying a Polo shirt vs buying a no-name shirt. They both provide the same function and they can even look very similar, but the name brand shirt usually costs a little more than the no-name shirt.

You may be quick to say, *"I think I'll just buy the generic bars and get more silver and gold for my money."* That would be true and that would be fine to do, in most circumstances. Similar to the government issued coins, not always, but typically when you go to sell, you will make back the premium that you paid for the name brand bar.

Also, another very important thing to keep in mind when you want to sell your generic bars is, who will you sell them to. The dealer you bought them from does not always have the best prices when you go to sell your bars back, so you may want to sell them to a different dealer to get a higher price. That dealer you try to sell them back to may or may not wish to buy them back from you. It depends on the dealer, the markets, the demand, the conditions and the prices.

This is not very common, but counterfeiters have drilled holes in some of the larger bars, filled the holes with cheap filler metals, and then covered up the outside holes with the real metal. Dealers can usually quickly spot this by weighing the bars however it is possible, not likely but possible, that a dealer could require the bar to be assayed before the dealer agrees to buy it from you. An assay is a test to ascertain the fineness and weight of a precious metal. If an assay is required, the seller usually has to pay for the cost of the assay.

As fabrication technology continues to improve, we are hearing more and more about counterfeiters altering bullion bars and even some coins, mostly coming out of China. Keep two things in mind on this. If and/or when the price of metals starts to really climb higher, that provides a lot more motivation for these counterfeiters to really ramp up production. And, once it starts becoming more frequent, assay test may also become more frequent. Yes, it's true that they can counterfeit name brand bars just as easy as generic bars. However, if you were going to counterfeit bullion bars, would you choose to counterfeit name brand bars that have serial numbers on them that can sometimes be authenticated and are often produced to higher standards, or would you rather counterfeit generic bars?

Like I said before, this is not typical and is more likely when you are dealing with larger size bars, but it is something that you should know before making your buying decisions. Even if you are selling your bars yourself on EBay or Craig's List. It's one thing to say, *"I have a generic 100 ounce silver bar"* and it's a different thing to say, *"I have a 100 ounce Engelhard silver bar with a serial code number."* If you were given the choice, which one would you prefer to buy?

To me I always feel better about buying name brand bars from very reputable mints that are known and trusted worldwide. To me it's like that insurance policy. Since there are so many uncertainties in about the future, I just feel better knowing that I have a name brand item that is widely recognized.

What Size Bars Should You Buy

Here are some things to keep in mind when deciding on the right size of bars to buy.

Space: From a space stand point, the larger the bar, the more compact and efficient it is for storage purposes. If you're main goal is to get as much value as possible into as small of space as possible, then the larger the bars, the better.

Value: If your main objective is to get as much gold and silver for your dollar, then typically the larger the size of the bar, the lower the premium or margins and you end up paying a lower cost per ounce. Remember the cupcake and sheet cake example?

Divisibility and Usability: The downside to owning larger bars is that you cannot break them up into smaller sizes and sell them as needed. It's an all or nothing thing. If you need to barter or trade with them, you are stuck with the value of that size bar. If, hopefully, the prices of gold and silver end up going to the moon, then the value of your bars is going to be really high. You don't want to have to walk down to your neighborhood grocery store with a 100 ounce bar of silver in your pocket looking to trade it out for some bread and milk. I'm sure you get the picture.

Salability: Typically speaking, the smaller the size bar, the easier it is to sell. This is not always the case and it totally depends on who you are selling to, what the market conditions are at the time, etc. If you are trying to sell a large bar back to a local dealer or to a local buyer, they may not have that much cash and may not want to buy back that much at that time, so a larger bar could possibly limit your sales options. If you are selling back to a large company, that should not be a problem.

As you have probably already figured out by now, the best answer is to diversify. Buy some smaller bars, some mid-size bars and some larger bars. That way you can spread out your risk.

Numismatic Coins

Okay, you have probably heard of numismatic coins but perhaps aren't totally sure what they are. Let's start with the definition. Numismatic coins are a type of coin that typically has a higher value than the face value and metal content of the coin itself, due to the history of the coin, the rarity, the grade, the age, and the condition of the coin. These are considered collectable coins.

Did you know that the US Mint estimates that there are around 140 million coin collectors in the USA alone? That's almost half of the population. Amazing. Collecting coins can be fun, educational, interesting and very profitable if you know how to do it right. In fact, the largest and nicest mansion I have ever been in is owned by a guy who started collecting coins when he was a kid, and then it just kind-of got out of hand. He amassed a huge fortune from numismatic and collectable coins.

With so many coin collectors in the world, it's easy to understand how really rare coins, in excellent condition can be worth so much. The most expensive coin sold was a 1933 Saint-Gaudens Gold Double Eagle that sold for $7,590,020. In 1991 if you had bought an MS 70 NGC Silver Eagle coin it would have cost you probably less than $30. Today it's worth over $5,000. Do all numismatic coins go up that much? Of course not.

1933 Saint-Gaudens Gold Double Eagle that sold for $7,590,020

1991 MS 70 NGC Silver Eagle worth over $5,000

Most numismatic coins are graded by licensed numismatists. The accepted global grading scale for rare coins is called the Sheldon Grading Scale. It goes from a 1 (which is the poorest quality of all), to a MS 70. MS stands for Mint State and a MS 70 is as high as the scale goes. An MS 70 is considered a *"perfect"* condition, uncirculated coin. Most graded coins are placed in a clear plastic, protective case, often called a slab. Many slabs come with a label that indicates the name and date of the coin, the grade and many also have a bar code and a hologram on them to help authenticate them.

Many people collect numismatic coins because they simply enjoy collecting the beautiful and rare coins. They get pleasure from collecting them and often hold on to them and pass them along to their children and/or grandchildren. Others buy them for the hope of making a high profit return on their investment. You certainly have the possibility of making a lot from these coins, but just like most things, the more knowledgeable you are, the greater your chances of being successful. It is very important to do your homework and really know what you are doing before you just walk into a dealer and ask him what he suggest you purchase.

Be aware that there are many "bullion only" people who hate numismatic coins, think they are the worst investment ever, and would not touch them with a 10-foot pole. Sure, if you don't know what you are doing and if you don't deal with knowledgeable and reputable dealers, you can really get taken advantage of. Not all numismatic coins will go up in value and some actually drop in value. However, some have appreciated much, much more than the bullion itself has.

Here is my take on this. Generally speaking, most human beings like to collect stuff. All kinds of stuff. Much of what most people collect is not necessarily profitable, but they just enjoy collecting stuff. I can promise you this, there is a ton of other stuff out there that you can choose to collect, that will never be near as valuable as numismatic coins.

If you enjoy collecting and like learning about coins, I think there is a place in your portfolio for them. However, unless you are an absolute expert in numismatics, I suggest you have only a small percentage of your investable assets in these coins. (More on this in the next chapter.)

You cannot rely on being able to sell these coins quickly, at the price you want, so don't look at them as a highly liquid investment. Typically these are long-term investments designed to be held for quite a while. Worst case scenario, they will always be worth the value of the metal content, which is a lot more than you can say about collecting other stuff. Best case scenario, they could end up being much more valuable and being a great investment for you.

Junk Silver

If you don't know what junk silver is, junk silver is an informal term used in the United States, United Kingdom, Canada and Australia for any silver coins that are in fair condition and have no numismatic or collectible value above the bullion content value of the silver that the coin contains. The word "junk" refers only to the value of the coins as collectibles and not to the actual condition of the coins. Also, junk silver is not necessarily scrap silver. Junk silver coins are not 99.9% pure silver, instead they typically range from 35% to 90% or more of pure silver, and the remaining amount of the coin is made up of various types of metal alloys. Thus they are not pure silver coins.

The most common junk silver U.S. coins were minted prior to 1965 and includes coins like:

Dollars – US Morgan and Peace dollars containing 90% silver, minted from 1878 to 1935

Half Dollars – Pre 1965 US Liberty Head "Barber," Walking Liberty, Franklin and Kennedy half dollars containing 90% silver. [Kennedy Half-Dollars (1965-1970, 1976) contain 40% silver]

Quarters – Pre 1965 US Liberty Head "Barber," Standing Liberty and Washington quarters containing 90% silver

Dimes – Pre 1965 Liberty Head "Barber," Winged Liberty Head "Mercury" and Roosevelt dimes; and Jefferson "Wartime" nickels containing 90% silver

Nickels – War Nickels (1942-1945 contain 35% silver)

How Junk Silver Is Sold

Most junk silver is purchased in canvas bags and is sold based on the <u>face value</u> of the coins. For example, if you purchases a $1,000 face value bag of US Mint 90% silver coins and you added up the denomination value of the coins, it would add up to $1,000. In other words, it would be like, $.25 + $.25 + $.10 + $.50 + $.25 would equal a face value of $1.35. However, the actual value of the $1,000 bag of junk silver is not $1,000, but actually a great deal more, because the silver content of the coins is much higher than the denomination value of the coins.

A $1,000 face value bag of US Mint 90% silver coins contains roughly 715 troy ounces of pure silver. The bags are usually comprised of 90% silver half dollars, quarters, dimes or a combination of these coins. At the time I am writing this, a $1,000 face value bag of junk silver actually costs almost $19,000. Depending on who you purchase from, you can usually buy bags with face values of; $50, $100, $250, $500, $1,000 and more.

Why Would You Want To Invest In Junk Silver?

Many people buy these coins as a form of insurance against the collapse of the dollar or our paper fiat currency. Even if the dollar were to collapse, these coins would still retain value because of the silver content that they contain. These coins, and precious metals in general, make great hedges against inflation. For example, in the 1960s a 90% silver quarter was worth $.25. Today it is worth about 20 times more or almost $5.00.

Junk silver is also a great option to use for barter if we get to the place in time where we need to barter. These coins maintain their value, they are small in size and weight, and they are low in their fractional denomination, so they are excellent to barter with for lower priced items. They are also legal US tender so at the very least, they are always worth their denomination face value.

You may remember back in the Jimmy Carter days of high inflation. Interest rates were sky high, inflation was soaring, silver and gold prices were soaring and we had the long gas lines all over America. Gas was hard to get and it was expensive. A small number of smart and resourceful gas station owners took advantage of this situation. They offered customers with 90% silver coins an opportunity to jump to the front of the long gas line, as long as they paid for their gas with these coins. Some even offered discounts on the price of gas if you paid with 90% silver coins. The gas station owners made a bundle and helped some of their customers as well.

Reasons Not to Go Overboard When Buying Junk Silver

If you ever go to resell your junk silver back to a broker / dealer, they sometimes pay much less for it than what you bought it for. So just from a pure investment standpoint, it is not always the best investment value. Also, these canvas bags of junk silver are very heavy, very bulky and take up a lot of space. The $1,000 face value bag we talked about above weighs about 55 pounds. If you plan to keep them in a safe, you had better get a very large safe. If you do not buy or sell your junk silver locally, the shipping costs to ship it back and forth can be very expensive. Also, if you are looking for a "portable" means of wealth, junk silver is near the bottom of the list. If you had to fill up your pockets with metals and leave in a hurry, you can certainly put a lot more value of pure bullion coins in your pockets than you could with junk silver.

In my opinion, I think it is find to own some junk silver and that it has its place in your metals investment portfolio, but I would not go crazy buying it.

You're Investment Pyramid

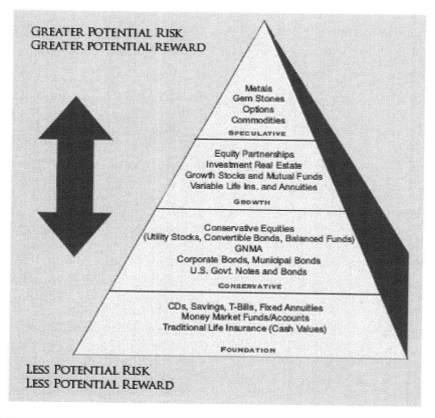

If you have ever worked with a financial planner or investment advisor before, you have probably heard of the Invest Pyramid. This is simply a portfolio investment strategy that allocates assets according to the relative safety and soundness of the investments. The bottom of the pyramid (the largest part) is usually comprised of low-risk investments, the middle portion is comprised of growth investments, and the top of the pyramid is usually comprised of more speculative investments. Below is a picture of a typical, traditional investment pyramid.

As you know, the actual pyramids in Egypt have lasted for thousands of years and stood the test of time. The pyramid investment concept helps you to limit your risk. Your core, less volatile investments are on the bottom, your minimal risk investments that have a good chance of growth are in the middle, and your higher risk, higher reward investments are at the top. This way, if your high risk investment bites the dust, you will still have most of your investments in the base and middle part of your pyramid and protect yourself financially.

As you can see, this pyramid has "Metals" listed at the very top. That is because most traditional investment advisors consider metals to be a risky investment. Where you choose to place metals in your overall portfolio is clearly up to you. Here is what I would argue about this point however. Most of these investment pyramids were created by people who "sell" the majority of the financial instruments shown in the pyramid. Most of these pyramids were created during "normal" economic times. These days there are very large numbers of people who have little trust in paper "fiat" currencies and put much more trust into physical metals.

Also, it does not take a rocket scientist to figure out that since global interest rates have been keep artificially low for so long, at some point interest rates have to jump up just up like a coiled spring, that's been artificially kept low for years. Many experts believe that metals will soar as interest rates move higher and the value of the dollar diminishes. This is a very extreme example, but it has been said that at the highest point of hyperinflation in post WWII Germany, you could have purchased an entire city block in the heart of downtown Berlin for just 25, ounce gold coins. At that time of hyperinflation it costs 200,000,000,000 paper German marks just to buy a single loaf of bread.

Like all of the options laid out in this book, it is up to you to choose how your investment pyramid is structured and what percentage amount of precious metals belongs in your pyramid. Once you determine what amount of precious metals you should have in your overall investment portfolio, you then have to also decide which specific types of precious metals should be in your portfolio and in what amounts. This is where a lot of people get confused. It's kind of like having a precious metals pyramid inside of your overall portfolio pyramid.

Thus, I suggest you use a similar pyramid approach for your precious metals investing. Below you will see a precious metals pyramid that I created.

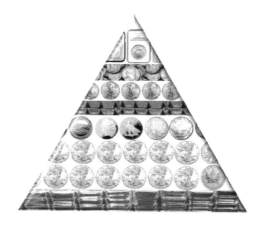

Precious Metals Pyramid

As I have stated throughout this book, each person's motivations, goals and means are different, and the makeup of the content of your precious metals portfolio should reflect your specific needs and abilities. You can build your pyramid any way you wish and, you do not necessarily need to start at the bottom first, and build up. You can purchase any parts of the pyramid you wish, at any time, while keeping an *"end plan"* in mind of how you want your metals pyramid to eventually look once it's complete. The above precious metals pyramid gives you an idea of one way to construct your pyramid. Here are my reasons for constructing the pyramid the way it is.

Silver bars make up the bottom base of the pyramid and can serve as a great foundational base after you have other core parts in place. Silver Eagles (or your own Government's coins) make up a large portion because they are so useful, liquid and all-round excellent investment. Next comes silver rounds. After you have your core holdings of government coins, you can then stock up on rounds if you wish.

I put gold bars next because they represent so much more value than our silver bars, and we need less of them to represent a great deal of value. Plus, depending on your view of the silver to gold value ratio and how you want to align your amounts of silver and gold, the amount of gold in your pyramid will vary. Gold Eagles (or your own Government's coins) come next as they represent great investments. Also, since I personally believe silver has much more growth potential due to the historical silver/gold ratio, I have much more silver than gold in the pyramid. Junk silver is next. It's good to have a portion of this in the pyramid, just not a ton of it in my opinion. Lastly comes the numismatic coins. I believe they do have a place in the pyramid/portfolio, but for most people, I think their place should be at the top.

Have some fun with this. Analyze your own needs and goals and sketch out how your own precious metals should look. Then go to work building your own pyramid and build it to last for the ages.

Where's The Best Place to Buy Metals From

Now comes the really important part. Where is the best place to buy your precious metals from? That is a really important question and the question that EVERYONE wants to know. If you do this right, you will be really happy. If you get this wrong, your metals investing experience can be very painful and frustrating.

It helps to know what kind of a shopper you are. Some people are hard core value or "deal" shoppers. They have got to find a killer deal, or they won't buy. Others are convenience shoppers. They don't much care what they pay for things as long as the shopping experience is smooth and easy. My suggestion for buy precious metals, is to be somewhere in the middle.

The Downside of Finding "Too Good To Be True" Deals

Most of the killer, low price deals out there are usually found when buying at garage sales, on Craig's List, EBay, the newspaper, etc. If you have plenty of time and patience, you can shop around and try and find a great deal, usually from an unsophisticated seller, who doesn't know the value of what they are selling. And yes, occasionally you can find a good deal here and there. However, there are a ton of downsides with this kind of shopping. If you need to buy a large quantity of metals, this way of shopping can take you a really long time. Plus, it is not very safe. If you arrange to meet the stranger from Craig's List, it can be very risky. When you show up with the cash at the "meet" location, what's to keep someone from knocking you in the head and taking your cash? It happens, and I don't think it is worth the risk. The other big risk with this method is that you have a much greater possibility of buying counterfeit precious metals this way.

Counterfeit Precious Metals

It used to be that coming across counterfeit precious metals was a rare occasion. However, times have changed. The technology and manufacturing equipment that is used to counterfeit coins and bars has improved so much, it is now much easier for bad guys to produce them. The fake ones are getting better and better quality wise, and they are becoming much harder to identify. Even experienced coin dealers are falling prey to some of these high quality counterfeit metals that are being dumped on the market.

Much of the counterfeit coins and bars are being produced in China. They can produce high quality "fake" gold and silver coins and small bars at a cost to them of only around $.50 each. The margins they can make are staggering and they can pump these fakes out 24/7 in gigantic quantities. To understand how this works, it's helpful to think like the bad guys think. The first thing most of them do is ship them out of the country. They typically do not target the large precious metals broker dealers, because generally speaking, the larger the dealer, the more likely they are to have experts on staff and have the latest counterfeit detection equipment available.

Consequently they usually target the "little guys" because they are usually looking for a killer deal and often do not have the expertise and equipment to detect the counterfeit items. A good portion of the counterfeit items get filtered down to flea market venders, Craig's List and EBay sellers and the like. They turn around and offer killer low prices on these shiny pieces of fake gold and silver and often it's the value, got-to-find-a-deal shopper who ends up buying these fakes. After the purchase is made, if the buyer were to determine that the item was a fake, it is often impossible to locate the seller or have any recourse for getting your money back. In these cases, what started out looking like an awesome deal, turns out to be a disaster.

For this reason, I personally believe that the safest way to shop is to buy from established and reputable bullion dealers. Yes, it's possible that a reputable dealer could come across some counterfeit metals but the odds of this happening are a LOT less and if they do, if they are truly reputable they will stand behind it and reimburse you or get you the real metals. That is the value of buying from a larger, more established company instead of the guy at the flea market.

However, you STILL need to be very cautious here. Some of the larger and more established broker dealers are great to work with and some of them will rip you off like you can't imagine, by charging sky high prices. Yes, I know it can be very frustrating and there are no easy shortcuts in the beginning if you don't already have a great bullion dealer whom you work with. There is no substitute to shopping around, asking a ton of questions and using your good judgment and intuition.

It pays to be open-minded. I have talked with countless people who sear up and down that they absolutely love their metals dealer and they get the best prices anywhere from their guy. They love "their guy" and they never even consider looking anywhere else. This can be a good thing however, more times than not, I find out that these guys are paying more than they should and don't even know it because they are not open-minded enough to shop around from time to time.

Watch Out For the Hidden Fees & Sneaky Sales Practices

Please don't get me wrong here. There are some precious metals broker dealers who are excellent to work with. They put your needs ahead of theirs and always act in your best interest and offer excellent products at very fair values. However, for everyone like that out there, you will find tons of them that will truly take advantage of you if they can. That is why I want to arm you with this information so you can recognize this and not be taken advantage of. It can be like swimming in shark infested waters, so you really need to watch your back and be smart.

There are over 10,000 precious metals broker dealers in the USA alone. The typical markup margin amount that they charge above what they paid for the metals usually ranges from 5% to over 40%. Don't ever forget this. Precious metals are commodities. *That's it!* There is NO REASON to pay a lot more for bullion than you have to. If you pay a 40% margin when you buy, you will NOT get it back when you go to sell and it will take you a lot longer to realize a profit on your purchase. So it truly pays to shop around and get good prices.

Here is another very important thing that you really need to be aware of. The business model and method of operation that some dealers use is to offer and promote lower upfront prices on certain "loss leader" items to get you to come into the store or get you to call or click. "That's the hook." This is similar to your local grocery store leading with a loss leader. They offer milk or eggs at a super low price to get you in the store, and the you end up buying a lot of other things that the store has great profit margins on.

Metals dealers primarily use these methods two different ways. The first way is they will get you to call in about the low price on a certain item. Once you contact them, they will do everything under the sun to get you to buy their other high margin items. I have been a sale/marketing person my entire life and I can tell you that without a doubt, some of the finest, most influential salespeople I have ever seen in my life, were metals salespeople. Some of these people can get you to do things that you can't even imagine that you would do otherwise.

Another method that far too many dealers use is to hide many of their sneaky little add-on fees until the last click or two of your check out. Some dealers have more fees than a telephone company bill, (and that's saying something). You would think most people would just not accept them, but most people do. By that time, they have already locked in their price and they just feel it is too late to pull out… so they pay the fees anyway. Some dealers make the majority of their profits from these hidden fees so you really need to identify them in advance, and this is not always easy, but it is definitely worth it.

Buying Local vs Buying Online or by Phone

Some people get overly fixated on the need to buy local. They feel that have to see, feel and touch "their" metals before they buy them, and they feel that if they buy online, or on the phone from a non-local company, they are taking a huge risk of never getting their metals or getting fake metals. I say, hogwash. It's simply not true. Yes, you may be able to find a local dealer who is great to work with, always has a great selection and has excellent prices. If that's the case, then by all means buy from them.

The entire precious metals business is Volume Based. If you are a small dealer and you can only afford to buy in small quantities, then you are going to pay higher wholesale prices for your metals. That's simply the way it works. It's unusual for a small local dealer to be able to get great wholesale prices and then sell to you at great prices. That is why, most of the time, the national dealers generally have lower prices. It's simply because they can buy at lower prices. They don't all pass those price savings along to their customers, but some do.

Dollar Cost Averaging

This is really important so please don't skip over this. I can't begin to tell you how many people I have had tell me that they were going to go *"all in"* with their first metals purchase. Seriously I have had people who have never bought one single piece of bullion in their life, tell me they were going to buy a half a million dollars' worth right away. Like we said in the beginning, a lot depends on how much investment capital you have. If you have many millions to invest in metals, then possibly buying that much at one time is okay, but if you don't have that kind of capital, then don't do it.

Occasionally I will get a call from someone and they are so excited. They just read a book or watched a video or talked with a respected advisor. The light bulb just came on in their head. They just learned what has really been going on in the economy. They just saw the stats on how many paper fiat dollars the Federal Reserve is printing and realize what's happening to the real value of those fiat dollars. They are new, they are inexperienced, they are excited, they are motivated, and they are often scared. They know they need to get some precious metals and they need to get some fast! They aren't sure what to buy, where to buy or how to buy, but they are ready to go ALL IN right now.

I always advise them to slow down and create a plan before they do anything. Also, I advise them to dollar cost average into and out of the market. Here is the thing. I don't care who you are or how smart you may be or think you are, no one can consistently, accurately predict the short term moves of the metals markets. No one! The gold markets are volatile and the silver market can be very volatile. Just about every time I used to try and guess, study, analyze and predict the short term price moves, I was wrong. I have a friend who has been in the metals markets for over 35 years. He is very smart, very well connected, and he owns thousands of dollars' worth of very expensive metals market forecasting and trading software. Even he gets it wrong more often than he gets it right. Trying to predict the short term price moves is very difficult.

Just like a competent equities investment advisor would advise you to dollar cost average your purchases of stocks or mutual funds, etc., the exact same wisdom holds true for metals. Here is a good way to do it that many people use. First determine the amount of funds that you plan to invest into metals. If it happens to be a really small amount, you do need to take transaction and shipping fees into account so you may not be able to dollar cost average near as much as someone with a larger amount.

If you have a decent amount of funds to invest in metals, then decide on a time frame that works for you. Some people choose 6 months, some choose a year, some choose 3 months, etc. Then simply take the amount you have to invest, and divide it up into chunks and set up a general time frame for investing it. Some people strictly stick to that time frame and buy at their pre-determined time regardless. Other people watch the markets and will make minor adjustments in their purchase times depending on price movements. If you do that, buy when it dips, not when it peaks. The overall important key is to be somewhat consistent and average your purchases out over time. If you do that, more times than not you will end up ahead of where you would be if you just went all-in.

The alternative is to simple guess that on this certain day and time is what you determine is the bottom of the market and you go all in with a single purchase of all your investable cash. If you are lucky and catch it perfectly, then you look like a genius. If you guess it wrong, then you look like a dummy. Don't be dummy. There is no reason to. I have lots of friends who simply buy metals all the time. Some buy most every week, or every two weeks or every month or every quarter, etc. It just depends on how much investable funds you have. It's good to have an accumulation mind set.

Here Is the Important Question to Ask Yourself

Regardless of what the current price of gold and silver is right now, do you believe sometime in the acceptable future that the prices will be much higher? If your answer is yes, then the short term price moves really don't matter that much. If you answered no, then you are probably investing in metals for different reasons, which is perfectly legitimate.

I get asked all the time, "Where do I think the price is going to go to." I have no idea. Some experts predict $5,000 gold and $500 silver and every other price target imaginable. I really have no idea myself but I do personally believe that at some time in the future, precious metals prices will be much, much higher than they are today. Personally I have learned not to sweat the short term price moves because I am not a trader. However, I do watch the markets. If the prices spike up dramatically, I have no problem selling some of my holdings and capturing some short term profits. Likewise, if the markets take a dramatic price dip, I usually use that as a buying opportunity.

What I have found is the less sophisticated metals investors tend to want to buy when the price spikes upwards and sell when the price dips down. All of the wiser veteran metals investors I know do just the opposite. They buy more when the price dips down and they sometimes sell when the price spikes up. Sometimes it take guts to do this, but most of the time it proves to be the winning strategy to follow.

Where to Store Your Metals

This is a very broad question and there is no one right answer. It depends on your personal wants and needs as well as your personal comfort level. It also depends on how much you have and where you live. If you live in a small apartment in Manhattan you may be more inclined to store your metals differently than someone who lives on some acreage in California. Obviously your personal safety should always be your number one concern.

Off Site Vault Storage Facilities

If you own or plan to buy a large amount of metals, you may want to consider using an offsite private vault storage facility to store your metals. Without a doubt, this is the most secure and safest way to store them. Keep in mind that this is also the most expensive way to store them, but it's the best. If you are on a budget this may not be your best option. When using offsite storage facilities there are two main types of storage; segregated and non-segregated. Segregated storage means that they will place the exact same metals that you have sent to them in a private container and tag them. When you go to request them to be sent to you or to a company whom you are selling them to, you will receive the exact same metals that you placed in storage.

With non-segregated storage, you will get the exact same quantity of metals that you placed in storage back, but it just may not be the exact same metals or it may not even be in the same form. You may place 10 monster boxes of silver eagle coins in storage, (10 boxes containing 500 one ounce coins each), and you may get back five 1,000 ounce silver bars. Non-segregated storage is typically less expensive than segregated storage. The good thing is, you can buy the metals from anywhere you wish and have them shipped directly to your storage vault without having to take physical possession of them yourself. As long as you choose a good facility, you metals will be totally safe and insured. You can also take them out anytime you wish.

If you would like to learn more about off-site vault storage, I have written an entire book on the subject titled: **How to Store Gold & Silver – The Complete Guide to Storing Gold & Silver in Off Site Vault Storage Facilities.** You can find more information on this in the Resources chapter at the end of this book.

Safes

Another great option is to invest in a high quality safe and keep them at your home or business. There are lots of tips and tricks on smart ways to store metals around your home or business. Here are a few tips on using a safe to store your metals. When choosing a safe, always go for quality. Why would you want to put a great deal of wealth and value in a cheap-o safe? However, people do it all the time. Find a way to secure your safe to a floor or wall. If you can cement it in, that's great. You can also bolt it to the floor or to a wall. Be sure to keep it out of site. If they can't find your safe, it's much harder for someone to rob it. Lastly, keep it to yourself. Don't' tell anyone about it.

If you can't decide on the best type of safe to get, here's a great tip. Call up an experienced safe cracker in your area. Someone who breaks into safes for a living. They can tell you the safes that are a complete waste of money and the ones they would use for themselves. A few minutes on the phone with the right guy can be invaluable to you. (Just don't tell him you plan to store a ton of gold and silver in your safe.)

Bury It

Believe it or not, a lot of wealthy people bury their metals on their property. The first time I heard of this I thought it was crazy but it's actually a great way to do it if it works for you. I know several people who have millions of dollars' worth of metals buried all over. Many people will get a 4 inch PVC pipe, put their metals inside, glue the other end on the pipe and be sure to bury it at least 4 feet deep, so it is deeper than most metal detectors can detect.

Safe Deposit Box

A lot of new metals investors first think of putting their metals in a local bank safe deposit box. It sure sounds like a great option at first. However, I really do not suggest that you do this. If the bank closes or goes out of business, your metals are tied up. Many people are not aware of this but with the new homeland security laws, they can actually take metals from your deposit box and they don't even have to notify you to do so. I know it seems odd, but this can be a very risky way to store your metals.

One of the single most important things about storing your metals is to keep the location of your metals to yourself. In most cases, it's best to tell no one at all. Really! If you don't want anyone to find your metals, then don't tell anyone where they are. Some people have a hard time getting their head around this and I do understand. Just remember that things have a way of changing. Businesses change, partnerships change, relationships change, circumstances change and more. What seems like a good idea today, may not be such a great idea down the road. I'm sure you've heard the military expression, *"Loose lips sink ships."* The expression came to be for a reason. It happens.

Finally, here is an important concept that you should know. I'm sure you will agree, these are the craziest economic times most of us have ever experienced. Who knows what tomorrow will bring. It is possible that we could all wake up one day and find that the world as we know it has turned up-side-down and things are no longer as they used to be. If that day were to come, you should be prepared for it. Regardless of where and how you plan to store your gold and silver, I suggest that you keep some of it, even if it's a small amount, in a location that you could get to within a short period of time if you needed to. This could be in your home or yard or office or somewhere, that you have complete control over and could access it within a short period of time.

While we don't know what the future holds, we do know that over time all fiat currencies have failed. We also know that over time, gold and silver have always maintained their value and have never failed. When times get tough, gold and silver always work. So be sure that you have some that you can get your hands on quickly, if you need to. Enough said.

The scope of this book does not allow me to go into a great deal of detail on this subject of metals storage. I have written a bestselling book called *"The Definitive Guide to Storing Gold & Silver"*. I believe it is the best and most comprehensive book on this subject. You can pick up a copy on Amazon very inexpensively. You can find more info on this in the Resources Chapter.

How to Track Your Precious Metals Value

Any wise investor always keeps a careful eye on their investments and they know how they are performing at all times. If you own stocks and mutual funds, you know how easy it is to keep track of your portfolio. You simply log into your Fidelity, Schwab or eTrade account, etc., and there you will see all of your equities and how they are performing to the minute. You can also see charts and graphs and other helpful information that helps you make wise decisions as to if you need to buy, sell, hold, etc.

When you start investing in precious metals, it's usually an entirely different story. Most investors buy some silver from one company, then months later buy some gold from a different company, then they buy some more silver later on, here and there, as funds allow.

They then have various paper receipts crammed together in a file somewhere that shows how much metals you bought, on what day, for what amount and what cost per ounce. All of your different purchases were made at different times, at different prices and for different metals products.

Then, you happen to catch the spot price of gold and silver in the paper, on a website or on the news. You see that the spot price has jumped way up or down and you and you say to yourself, perhaps this is a buying opportunity and I should buy some more. Or perhaps it is a selling opportunity and you should cash in some of your quickly earned profits.

The problem for most people is, they really have no idea of how much gold and silver they actually own at any one time. They don't know what the current value of their overall metals portfolio is at that time and they don't know what their average cost per ounce is for each metal group. Without this information, it is very hard to make a wise and informed buying or selling decision.

There are a few paid services out there that track your metals but I have yet to be impressed with any of them. A quick, easy and free suggestion is to just create an Excel spread sheet. Enter all of your purchases, the date you bought them, how much you paid and the total number of ounces of each item you bought, by metal type.

Then just create a simple Excel formula. You can enter the current spot price of each metal and have the formula automatically calculate and update the current value of your holdings.

Precious Metals for IRAs and 401Ks

It's amazing to me but there are so many people who have no idea that they can put physical gold and silver into their IRA, SEP, Roth and/or 401k. It's true. This is perfectly legal and allowed in the United States, IF you do it correctly. However, it needs to be a special kind of IRA. If your IRA or 401K is with Fidelity, Vanguard or any of the giant, main-stream brokerage companies, they are not set up for this and do not allow you to invest in physical precious metals. It's simply not possible with them.

If you call up your custodian or the company who maintains your IRA and/or 401k and tell them you want to buy physical precious metals with your investment funds, they will most likely do everything they can to talk you out of it. They will likely tell you that you can *"achieve the same thing"* by simply investing in precious metals ETFs, mutual funds, stocks, etc. Do you know why they will tell you that? I bet you do. Actually there are two reasons. The first reason is they do not have the ability to sell you physical precious metals and if you end up buying precious metals, they will make no money on them. Reason two is, if you buy their "paper" forms of gold and silver, they will make money on those when you buy and sell them. It's really that simple. Follow the money, it leads you to the motivations.

Please keep this in mind. You MUST do this correctly in order to avoid finding yourself in a big mess with the IRS and possibly losing your IRA tax exempt status and having to pay all kinds of fees and penalties. First off, you need to find an IRA custodian who handles investments in physical precious metals, and there are not a lot of them. In most cases you will have to open a separate IRA for your precious metals, fill out a lot of forms, pay some fees, etc. The IRS will not allow you to move metals that you already own into your new precious metals IRA, so you will need to make new purchases for this. Also, you are not allowed to have physical possession of *"most"* types of metals that can be held in your IRA account. They are typically held by a custodian or a depository. Most on this in a moment.

Mainly there are two different types of self-directed IRA platforms, the **Trust model** and the **Checkbook Control model**. The huge majority of "Gold IRA" programs that you see advertised are based on the Trust model. I'm sure you already guessed the reason why these guys spend so much on advertising. You got it... it's because they are very profitable to them. Some of you may be saying, *"But Doyle, how can they make any money on this because many of them offer to set up a gold IRA for you for $50 to several hundred dollars and yes, some are even offering to do this for free. Why would they do such a thing?"* Well, the **Trust model** allows the companies to charge a ton of fees. Fees like managerial fees, transaction fees, annual asset fees, wire fees, entrance and exit fees, purchase and sell fees, holding fees and much more.

It's not uncommon to have to pay thousands of dollars in fees, PER YEAR, on your *"free"* gold IRA. Plus, in addition to that, many of these Trust model companies dictate **where you buy** your metals from and dictate **where you store** your metals. And guess what, they often earn fees when you buy your metals and every month when you pay to store your metals. If you like paying never-ending fees, you will love the Trust model.

Thankfully there is a better way. The self-directed IRA based on the **Checkbook Control model** offers much, much more flexibility. Plus, there are no managerial or transaction fees. This model allows you to purchase your metals from anyone you choose and you can store your metals at any licensed depository you wish. This allows you the option to shop around and hopefully find lower prices. You can set up a Checkbook Control model IRA yourself, but there is lots of paperwork and it is pretty complicated. Unless you are an expert in this area, I would not recommend trying to go it alone.

Most investors opt to find a company who specializes in this, and who knows the forms, the laws, and all of the dos and don'ts inside and out. It's not unusual to spend several thousand dollars to get a checkbook control IRA set up correctly. However I have found that most investors end up paying more in fees the first year of a Trust model IRA than they will spend getting a checkbook control IRA set up. After the checkbook IRA is set up...the ongoing fees are very, very small. Plus, you can take the fees to set up your checkbook IRA out of your IRA funds if you wish, so that your out-of-pocket funds are minimal.

Another thing I totally love about the Checkbook Control model is that after you buy as much gold and silver as you deem sound for your portfolio, you can also invest in things like; residential and commercial real estate, raw land, trust deeds and mortgages, private notes and placements, LLCs, foreclosure property, receivables, stocks, bonds, mutual funds, currency, futures, commercial paper and much, much more. This puts the power and flexibility into your hands and allows you to invest in the best opportunities and in what you know best. You can't believe how easy it is. When you want to buy an approved asset in your IRA, you simply write the check. That's it. Hence the name, checkbook IRA.

Many investors these days want to invest in gold and silver but they are cash poor. They don't have a lot of liquid money sitting around to buy much metals with. However, most people do have a sizable IRAs and/or 401ks that they could buy the precious metals they want, if they structure a new precious metals IRA correctly.

What Types of Precious Metals Are Allowed In a Self-Directed IRA?

The current laws dictate that the gold must be .9950 pure gold and the silver must be .9990 pure silver, and both platinum and palladium must be .9995 pure to quality. If you prefer to buy bullion bars they must be fabricated by COMEX, NYMEX, or ISO 9000 approved refiners.

Some examples of acceptable forms of silver that is allowed to be held in an IRA are; American Eagle coins, America The Beautiful coins, Australian Kookaburra coins, Austrian Vienna Philharmonic coins, British Britannia coins (2013 and newer), Canadian Maple leaf coins, Chinese Panda coins, Mexican Libertad coins, and various bars and rounds that are .999 pure or more.

For Platinum, American Eagle coins, Australian Koala coins, Canadian Maple Leaf coins and various bars of .9995 purity are acceptable. For Palladium, Canadian Maple Leaf coins and various bars of .9995 purity are acceptable.

Can You Really Store Your IRA Gold & Silver At Home?

There seems to be quite a bit of confusion over this. Does the government really allow individuals to store the metals in their own self-directed IRA at their home or any place they choose? This is addressed in Section 408(m)(3)(B) of the Tax code. The code makes a distinction between what they term bullion and coins. For **bullion**, it must have a fineness level of .9950% for gold and .9990% for silver and the bullion must come from a COMEX, NYMEX or an approved refiner.

Section 408(m)(3)(A) contains the rules for **coins**. It says that most government manufactured gold and silver coins are acceptable. Popular examples include American Eagles, Canadian Maple Leafs, and Australian Nuggets. Section 408(m)(3)(B) of the Tax code states that **bullion** must be held "in the physical possession of a trustee". This is usually a specialized custodian and/or depository. For **coins**, the tax code has no such requirements. The code does not place any restrictions whatsoever on the storage requirements for gold and silver coins. Based on the tax law, your IRA can purchase gold and silver coins and you can hold them personally.

For many people, this news comes as a shock and a surprise. There are a few reasons for this. May people in the industry are simply not well versed in the IRS code. Another motivation out there is, most people who get paid a fee for storing your metals, will usually not go out of their way to let you know about the details of the tax code. So at least you have a choice when it comes to storing coins for your IRA. You can either store them with a custodian or in a depository, or you can store them in any place you deem safe. For many, having this option is a huge plus both cost wise and for their own piece of mind.

Just so you know, storage fees can really add up. Plus, they never go away until or unless you stop storing your metals. Many new investors are simply not aware of this expense and often overlook it or do not consider it. If home storage may be right for you, this option could save you a lot of money and enable you to purchase more metals instead of using those funds to pay for storage.

How to Choose the Best Company to Set Up Your Precious Metals IRA?

As with everything, it always pays to shop around and do your research to find the company that is right for you. Just like we have said so many times before, always remember to get all of your questions asked upfront. Unfortunately many companies do not tell you about all of their fees up front and if you don't ask, they you will likely find out the hard way.

Often I do get asked who I used to set up my self-directed checkbook control IRA with. As you may imagine, I did tons and tons of research (over about 2 years) before I finally decided on the company to use, and ended up getting a really good education in the process. I found a company whom I am delighted with, who met all of my needs and were very affordable to me. In the resources section of this book you can find the contact information for the company I use and recommend.

When to Sell and How to Sell

I'm sure you have heard the term Gold Bug. If not, it's typically refers to someone who buys and holds onto gold forever. I totally get that and understand that. If that is you and you plan to just buy and buy and buy... and never sell, then that is perfectly well and good. For me, I am more of a wealth cycles investor. I prefer to invest in asset classes that are in an upwards growth cycle. Consequently I think there are times to buy metals and there are times to sell them. The time to sell metals may not be for a really, really long time. We'll just have to see how things pan out. For many of us, we realize that there will be times to sell at least some of our metals and take some easy profits.

I strongly encourage you not to adopt a "day trader" mentality with physical metals. The actual physical metals are just too cumbersome to actively buy and sell within very short periods of time. If you want to trade the short term moves of the metals markets, I suggest you either buy or sell the ETFs, mining stocks, mutual funds, commodities, or other forms of more liquid precious metals. You will make yourself crazy and be eaten up by fees if you try and buy and sell physical metals like a day trader.

As long as you paid attention to the chapters above and purchased the right types of metals, you will find that they are really easy to sell. They are very liquid investments and people all around the world will buy your metals from you if you have what they want. If you get to a place where you want to sell some of your metals but think it will be too hard or too much of a hassle, then you need know this. When you get ready to sell your metals, just do it. It's easier than you might think.

When you need to sell some of your metals, here are some important things to keep in mind. First off, the "buy" price that you can get for your metals varies as much or more as the "sell" price did when you were shopping to buy your metals. You should shop around just as hard for the best price when you go to sell, as you did when you bought your metals. You will be amazed at how much the prices can vary. Some of the dealers out there have a "some-what" similar mentality as the "We Buy Gold" people do. They will offer you the absolute lowest price that they possibly can, and try and take advantage of the unsophisticated metals seller. There are tons of them out there, and that's why the "we buy gold" people make so much money. I don't want you to be one of those victims. There's no reason to be a victim when you are armed with the right information.

Most dealers will set there buy back prices at so much above or below spot price. That's your benchmark to compare to. Don't just ask a dealer what they will pay for a tube of silver eagles. Ask them how much above or below spot price they will pay for a tube of silver eagles. That way, as the spot price changes while you are shopping around, you will have a constant benchmark to compare to.

Keep in mind that different types of metal items will have different buy back margins. Bars will be different from coins. Different types of coins will usually have different buy back margins as well. It's all about supply and demand. If the demand for a certain item is high, then you will typically get more for it and vice versa.

If you are selling to a non-local company, (which is a perfectly fine thing to do), be sure to ask them about ALL of the fees that will be involved. Similar to what we talked about in the chapter: 'Where's The Best Place to Buy Metals', some dealers will offer you a great price up front for your metals and then make their profits by adding on a ton of little hidden fees that only pop-up at the very end. Remember; ask, ask and ask some more.

Another very important thing to ask them is <u>when</u> will the buyback price be locked in? Some dealers will lock it in when you are on the phone with them and you agree to sell back to them. Most will not lock it in until they actually receive the metals you send to them. Either way can be fine depending on the price that you agree to, but just be sure you are clear on this. A small number of dealers will allow you to send your metals back to them without first locking in a price, and then they will agree to hold them for you for a certain amount of time, and you can call and lock in a sale price at any time you wish during that time period. This option gives you more control to try and catch the very best possible price.

Be sure to ask them for the exact address it needs to be sent back to, how it should be sent back, who pays the shipping and insurance, etc. Always ship your metals in a way that is traceable and insured. Many people use FedEx, UPS and some will use the US Post Office. Don't be cheap here. Spend the money to insure you are sending it in the safest and quickest way. Also, be sure to ask the dealer when and how your will be paid for your metals. Believe it or not, this varies quite a bit and some dealers hold onto your money for quite a while.

Time to Take Action

Okay, if you are still with me I'm sure you have learned a great deal by now. I'm sure you remember the saying, *"Knowledge is only power when the knowledge is used."* The same principal holds true here. It's time to get into the game and take action. I'm not saying you need to go out and make a purchase today, but you should start creating and refining your plan if you have not already done so. Set your metals investing goals. Sketch out your precious metals pyramid and determine what you want yours to look like. Start shopping around and searching for the right broker dealers to use when you are ready to buy. Think about where you plan to store your metals and start working on that plan.

Yes, there is lots to do and it does take some time and effort. As with everything, the most difficult part is in the beginning. As you start to figure things out I promise you it will become easier and easier. The key is not to give up. It's worth it to persist. Don't give up and see your plan through to completion. If you don't know something, ask. The answers are out there. Just be careful who you ask. Look at their motivations and weigh them against their answers. Try and determine whose best interest they have in mind.

Also, if you are still not clear on what types of metals are best for you, remember you are not making an irrevocable decision. You can always sell what you have and buy other things. Gold and silver are very liquid commodities and they are easy to buy and sell. Remember, you can't go wrong buying Government issued coins and/or most quality name brand items. If you are new and unclear what to buy, then don't buy the unusual or non-main stream items. They are harder to buy and sell. Stick to the basics until you grow in knowledge and experience and then you can branch out into other areas.

You will no doubt have some family members and friends who think you are a little crazy for wanting to buy bullion. Don't listen to them. They are just uneducated in this area and don't understand it. Most people are critical about things that they don't know and understand. That is why it's best to keep your metals investing to yourself and let others mind their own business.

Thanks for investing your time and energy into reading this book. It is my sincere desire that this book has been a blessing to you and saved you from a lot of potential heart aces and lost funds. I wrote the type of book that I wish I would have had when I first started out. If I would have known then, what I know now, I would have avoided doing a lot of stupid things and would have saved myself a lot of resources. If you can avoid just some of the pitfalls by having read this book, then I am fulfilled.

I wish you the very best in your precious metals investing.

All the best to you.

Thanks so much and God Bless.

Doyle Shuler

CEO, Multiple Streams Marketing, LLC

info@MultipleStreamsMarketing.com

Resources

I have been investing in precious metals for almost 30 years. Over that time, I've seen a lot of good things and regrettably, I've seen a lot of very, very bad things in the industry. I've seen people lose their life savings, and even seen some lose their homes, and the homes of their loved ones, by making really bad choices. In the early years, I had no one to guide me and steer me towards the good options. I had to learn by trial and error and believe me, there was lots of *"error"* and it always costs me dearly. It doesn't have to be that way for you.

Below are some resources that I think are excellent and believe you will find very helpful. In fact, I personally use all of these resources myself. Noted, I am an affiliate or owner of these items and should you decide to purchase any of them through my links, I will make a commission on them. However, my philosophy has always been to treat everyone as I would myself, so I *only* make available the resources that I truly believe are *"best in class"* and ones that offer excellent values.

Gold Silver Alliance

A lot of people ask me where I buy my gold and silver from. Over the years, I've made purchases from many, many different broker/dealers around the country, all with varying results. I've always wanted to have my own gold and silver company so I could do things the right way and treat people the way they deserve to be treated. I became so tired of all the games and shady sales tactics that far too many dealers use to take advantage of metals investors every day. Over the years, I've been fortunate to develop friendships with some really exceptional people who have top level connections with the largest metals wholesale suppliers in the world. We decided to form our own precious metals company that offers a new approach to metals investing.

We are a group of seasoned gold & silver professionals who believe in offering a fresh, new, bold approach to precious metals investing. The Gold Silver Alliance was formed to provide an easier and more affordable way for metals investors to buy and sell metals. The Alliance is a group of like-mined, value conscious, independent thinkers, who have the courage and wisdom to take the actions that are necessary to insure our own success.

You will love our Concierge Club. It's free to join and comes with tons of FREE member benefits. We treat our Concierge Club members the same way we like to be treated ourselves. We don't surprise you with hidden fees that pop-up out of nowhere. We don't bait-and-switch our members by luring them in with low advertised prices and then hard-sell them on items that are more profitable to us.

We operate with trust and integrity. It's who we are. Our philosophy is; *If we can offer our Alliance Members superb values and some of the smartest, seldom seen investment options on the planet, you will tell others about us and help us grow the Alliance.*

We offer value. We don't use high pressure, commissioned sales people. We don't spend millions on TV advertising and we don't pay movie stars to promote our company. We take those savings and funnel them back to our members in the form of more affordable prices. This allows us to offer our metals at prices that will make you smile. Our concierge associates will answer your questions and carefully guide you to the metals that are in your best interest and that offer the best values.

Our management team has over a half of century of experience in the precious metals industry. We have long standing relationships with some of the largest wholesale metals companies in the world. Due to our high level of metals purchases, we are able to purchase from our wholesalers at the lowest price levels they offer. That's how we provide value for our Alliance members.

Head over to GoldSilverAlliance.com right now. Sign up for free. Check out all the free benefits you get just for showing up. Check out our LOW prices. *You'll be glad you did.*

Barefoot Retirement Plan

You've probably heard of the old parable that talks about... *If you find something really good, you want to share it with your friends*, right? Well, that's how I feel about this program. This program is a true, *"Game Changer."* Once you understand just how unique and powerful it is, it truly has the ability to dramatically impact your life for the better! I share this with you for two important reasons.

First, this unique and *"little known"* program offers an optional way to buy precious metals, and earn market indexed returns on the same funds you used to purchase your metals, at the same time. It's a unique way to use arbitrage, and "double dip" on your earnings, and really maximize your investment returns. Really amazing.

Second, it's one of the finest retirement programs ever created by man. No exaggeration. In fact, this is a relatively new (less than a year old), **patented program,** and it can only be offered by a very small number of select few experts. The actual concept has been used for over 150 years. This patented version of the program, reduces its cost by up to 70%, and makes it one of the best retirement options ever created.

Did you know that in a recent study, it was determined that 61% of Americans fear running out of money during retirement, more than they fear death itself? Plus, 87% of Americans are not confidant that they have saved enough for retirement! Man, those stats really shocked me, but they're true. And with all of the crazy ups & downs in the economy, our raging debt crisis, the health care debacle, global unrest, etc., it's easy to see why people are so frightened about this. After all, who wants to spend their retirement years as a Walmart greeter, right?

Here's the thing. This program is definitely not for everybody. It may not be your cup of tea, or you may not even qualify to participate in it, but I can certainly tell you this. Some of the wealthiest people in the country, and many of the largest companies in the country, are participating in this program in a BIG way because of the amazing value and benefits it offers. Some companies are literally putting tens of billions of dollars into programs like this.

In other words, if it was not such a fabulous program, these individuals and companies would certainly not be falling over themselves to take advantage of it. Of all the investment and retirement programs I have ever seen, in my entire life, this one is hands down, miles ahead of anything else out there! The benefits it offers are nothing short of *jaw-dropping!*

Here are just some of the benefits this amazing program offers: **100% Tax-Free income, guaranteed not to lose a penny due to**

market downturns, completely and totally private, can offer a life-time income, no contribution limits, one of the safest programs on planet earth, liquid and flexible, option to leverage and earn two different returns on the exact same funds, no investment restrictions, the lowest fees found anywhere.

Yep… I told you it was really amazing. And these are not even all of the benefits that the program offers.

If this sounds like something you would like to find out more about, we've put together an outstanding book that will show you exactly how it works, why it's so different from anything else out there, and how it may dramatically benefit you, your family, your business, and your loved ones.

You can purchase the book on Amazon. However, for a limited-time, we are making the eBook version of the book available *Totally Free!* I honestly don't know how long we will be able to continue making it free, but at the time of this writing, the book is totally and completely free on the website.

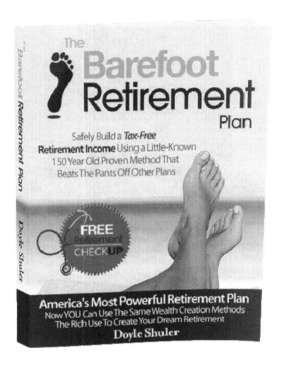

To grab your *FREE COPY* of The Barefoot Retirement Plan, go to:

www.BarefootRetirement.com

You'll be glad you did!

Plus, we are offering a
100% FREE Retirement CheckUP.

Similar retirement checkups cost $500 or more. **Ours is completely Free.** This is one of the finest retirement checkups on the market. It only takes a few minutes to enter in your information. You will receive a 17 page detailed report with color charts & graphs that will clearly show you if you're on track to reach your retirement goals.

Why worry about what your retirement will look like when you can find out for sure, in just a few minutes. And it won't cost you a cent.

To get your Retirement CheckUP while it's still 100% FREE, go to:

BarefootRetirement.com/CheckUP

___

SurvivalResources.org

I am fortunate to have quite a few high net worth friends. Want to know something that just about all of them have in common? They all have stocked up like crazy on survival resources of all types (including metals). These are not the crazy people you see on TV that live in the woods and are dooms day freaks.

These are multi-millionaires who can afford just about anything they want. They're smart people. They know that smart people have contingency PLANS. They plan for the worst, just in case it happens, so they will be prepared. They look at survival preparedness like they look at buying insurance. Prudent people buy insurance to protect themselves from the unexpected.

Anyone who is half-way paying attention to what's going on these days knows that we are truly living in unprecedented times. Things are happening today that none of us would have ever imagined just a hand full of years ago. So smart people prepare for the unexpected.

A buddy of mine is friends with a former Navy Seal. This guy lives and breathes survival preparedness and boy does he know his stuff. He recently spent several hours reviewing and demonstrating the core survival items that he deems as critical, must-have items. I was so impressed (and shocked) by what he had to say, I decided to create a website that contains all of the survival items he and other experts rely on themselves.

The site is: SurvivalResources.org There you will find all of his recommended items, all in one place. You won't have to scour the web and spend endless hours trying to figure out what's good and what is not. It's all here on this one site. It's like a one-stop-shop site, for all of the *"Navy Seal Recommended"* survival items you need. Check it out today. Be sure you and your family are fully prepared for the unexpected. Note; once you stock up on these items, you can't imagine how much better you will sleep at night.

Easy IRA Solutions

If you've not put at least some of your IRA or 401K funds into a physical gold and silver IRA and/or 401K, you are missing out on one of the best opportunities you will ever have in your lifetime! Many financial planners are now suggesting investors put 10% to 30% of their investment portfolio in physical gold and silver. There are only a handful of companies that allow you to have **physical gold and silver** in your IRA account.

Mainly there are two different types of self-directed IRA platforms, the **Trust model** and the **Checkbook Control model**. The huge majority of "Gold IRA" programs that you see advertised are based on the Trust model. The **Trust model** allows the companies to charge a ton of fees. Fees like managerial fees, transaction fees, annual asset fees, wire fees, entrance and exit fees, purchase and sell fees, holding fees and much more.

It's not uncommon to have to pay thousands of dollars in fees, PER YEAR, on your *"free"* gold IRA. Plus, in addition to that, many of these Trust model companies dictate **where you buy** your metals from and dictate **where you store** your metals. And guess what, they often earn fees when you buy your metals and every month when you pay to store your metals. If you like paying never-ending fees, you will love the Trust model.

Thankfully there is a better way. The **Self-Directed IRA** based on the **Checkbook Control model** offers much, much more flexibility. Plus, there are no managerial or transaction fees. This model allows you to purchase your metals from anyone you choose. Another big thing to consider is most IRA *"require"* you to store your metals in licensed depositories and many IRA custodians earn commissions on your storage fees forever. With the IRA program I found, they have the customer's best interest in mind and educate them about the fact that, if you purchase the right, Government IRA approved coins, the tax code does NOT place any restrictions whatsoever on the storage requirements for them. Based on the tax law, your IRA can purchase certain gold and silver coins and you can store them personally. This is a big, big deal and you can save a lot of money with this option if it's right for you.

The Self-Directed IRA allows you to shop around and find best prices for your metals and for your storage, if you choose to. Another thing I totally love about the Checkbook Control model is that after you buy as much gold and silver as you deem sound for your portfolio, you can also invest in things like; residential and commercial real estate, raw land, trust deeds and mortgages, private notes and placements, LLCs, foreclosure property, receivables, stocks, bonds, mutual funds, currency, futures, commercial paper and much, much more. This puts the power and flexibility into your hands and allows you to invest in the best opportunities and in what you know best. You can't believe how easy it is. When you want to buy an approved asset in your IRA, you simply write the check. That's it. Hence the name, checkbook IRA.

Many investors these days want to invest in gold and silver but they are cash poor. They don't have a lot of liquid money sitting around to buy much metals with. However, most people do have a sizable IRAs and/or 401ks that they could buy the precious metals they want, if they structure a new precious metals IRA correctly.

To find out more about how this unique and very profitable program works, go to: www.EasyIRASolutions.com

---

Where Should I Store My Precious Metals?

(**Note:** As an author, public personality and spokesperson on precious metals, I DO NOT keep any precious at my residence or office. All of my metals at stored at non-disclosed, off site vault storage locations.)

This is a question I get several times a week. It's not uncommon to have new metals investors buy 50K, 100K or several hundred thousand dollars right off the bat. Yes, there are a lot of people, buying LOTS of metals these days.

Lots of new investors have no idea of where or how to safely store the metals they buy. I have spent hundreds of hours talking with people about the multitude of options for storing their metals and the pros and cons of them. You probably guessed it by now, but I finally grew tired of spending so much of my time explaining this to people, so I wrote a book on the subject.

It's actually a BEST SELLER and I believe it's the most comprehensive book on the subject of storing precious metals that you will find anywhere. The book is available on Amazon. It's very inexpensive and I promise you will learn things about storing metals that you have never imagined before. And…since the safety issue is so big with gold and silver, this could be the most important book about metals that you ever read. Seriously. This subject is nothing to take lightly.

You can check it out on Amazon by going to:
http://safelink8.com/StorageBook

Disclaimers

Disclaimer and Terms of Use Agreement

This book was designed to provide information about the subject matter covered herein. It is distributed with the understanding that the author and the publisher are not engaged in rendering financial, legal, accounting, or other professional services. If financial, legal accounting or other professional advice or other professional assistance is required, the services of a competent professional advisor should be sought.

Efforts have been made to make this book as complete and accurate as possible. However, there may be mistakes both typographical and in content. Therefore, the texts should be used only as general guides and not as the ultimate sources of the subject matters covered.

The author and the publisher shall have neither liability nor responsibility to any person or entity with respect to any loss or damage caused or alleged to be caused directly or indirectly by the information covered in this report.

The author and publisher of this eBook, and the accompanying materials have used their best efforts in preparing this publication. The author and publisher make no representation or warranties with respect to the accuracy, applicability, fitness, or completeness of the contents of this book. The information contained in this book is strictly for educational purposes. Therefore, if you wish to apply any of the ideas contained in this book, you are taking full responsibility for your actions.

Every effort has been made to accurately represent this product and it's potential. Even though this industry is one that has a great upside profit potential, there is no guarantee that you will earn or save any money using the techniques and ideas contained in these materials. Examples in these materials are not to be interpreted as a promise or guarantee of earnings or savings. Earning and saving potential is entirely dependent on the person using this product and its ideas and techniques as well as market and economic conditions and fluctuations. We do not purport this as a get rich scheme. You could lose all of the money you invest in any investment. No one can predict the future nor market prices. You should only invest money that you can afford to lose and you should only invest after seeking council with your financial planner and/or advisor or other professionals in this field.

We cannot guarantee your success, savings or profits. Nor are we responsible for any of your actions.

Materials in our product and our websites may contain information that includes or is based upon forward-looking statements within the meaning or the securities litigation reform act of 1995. Forward-looking statements give our expectations or forecasts of future events. You can identify these statements by the fact that they do not relate strictly to historical or current facts. They use words such as "anticipate," "estimate," "expect," "project," "intend," "plan," "believe," and other words and terms of similar meaning in connection with a description of potential earnings or financial performance.

Any and all forward looking statements here or on any of our sales materials are intended to express our opinion of earnings or savings potential. Many factors will be important in determining your actual results and no guarantees are made that you will achieve results similar to ours or anybody else's, in fact no guarantees are made that you will achieve any results from our ideas and techniques in our materials.

The author and publisher disclaim any warranties (expressed or implied), merchantability, or fitness for any particular purpose. The author and publisher shall in no event be held liable to any party for any direct, indirect, punitive, special, incidental or other consequential damages arising directly or indirectly from any use of this material, which is provided "as is", and without warranties.

As always, the advice of a competent legal, financial, tax, accounting or other professional should be sought before taking any actions or making any purchases. The author and publisher do not warrant the performance, effectiveness or applicability of any sites listed or linked to in this book. All links are for information purposes only and are not warranted for content, accuracy or any other implied or explicit purpose.

This Book and all related materials are © copyrighted by Multiple Streams Marketing, LLC. No part of this may be copied, promoted or changed in any format, sold, or used in

any way other than what is outlined within this Book under any circumstances.

The End

Or Perhaps

The Beginning